PIANO | VOCAL | GUITAR • CD   VOLUME 1

HAL•LEONARD
ANO PLAY-ALONG

MOVIE MUSIC

T004842

CONTENTS

PAGE	TITLE	DEMO TRACK	PLAY-ALONG TRACK
2	Come What May **MOULIN ROUGE**	1	2
14	Forrest Gump – Main Title (Feather Theme) **FORREST GUMP**	3	4
18	My Heart Will Go On (Love Theme from Titanic) **TITANIC**	5	6
9	The Rainbow Connection **THE MUPPET MOVIE**	7	8
24	Tears in Heaven **RUSH**	9	10
29	A TIme for Us **ROMEO AND JULIET**	11	12
32	Up Where We Belong **AN OFFICER AND A GENTLEMAN**	13	14
36	Where Do I Begin **LOVE STORY**	15	16

ISBN 0-634-06900-4

HAL•LEONARD®
CORPORATION
7777 W. BLUEMOUND RD. P.O. BOX 13819 MILWAUKEE, WI 53213

Visit Hal Leonard Online at
www.halleonard.com

COME WHAT MAY

from the Motion Picture MOULIN ROUGE

Words and Music by
DAVID BAERWALD

THE RAINBOW CONNECTION

from THE MUPPET MOVIE

Words and Music by PAUL WILLIAMS
and KENNETH L. ASCHER

FORREST GUMP–MAIN TITLE
(Feather Theme)
from the Paramount Motion Picture FORREST GUMP

Music by ALAN SILVESTRI

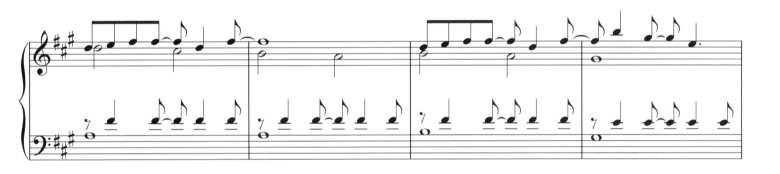

MY HEART WILL GO ON

(Love Theme from 'Titanic')

from the Paramount and Twentieth Century Fox Motion Picture TITANIC

Music by JAMES HORNER
Lyric by WILL JENNINGS

TEARS IN HEAVEN

featured in the Motion Picture RUSH

Words and Music by ERIC CLAPTON
and WILL JENNINGS

Would you know my name ___
Would you hold my hand ___
Would you know my name ___

if I saw you in heav - en?
if I saw you in heav - en?
if I saw you in heav - en?

Would it be the same ___
Would you help me stand ___
Would you be the same ___

Be - yond the door _____ there's peace, I'm sure, _

A TIME FOR US
(Love Theme)
from the Paramount Picture ROMEO AND JULIET

Words by LARRY KUSIK and EDDIE SNYDER
Music by NINO ROTA

UP WHERE WE BELONG

from the Paramount Picture AN OFFICER AND A GENTLEMAN

Words by WILL JENNINGS
Music by BUFFY SAINTE-MARIE and JACK NITZSCHE

WHERE DO I BEGIN

(Love Theme)
from the Paramount Picture LOVE STORY

Words by CARL SIGMAN
Music by FRANCIS LAI

PIANO PLAY-ALONG

THE ULTIMATE SONGBOOKS!

These great book/CD packs come with our standard arrangements for piano and voice with guitar chord frames plus a CD. The CD includes a full performance of each song as well as a second track without the piano part so you can play "lead" with the band.

VOLUME 1. MOVIE MUSIC

Come What May • Forrest Gump – Main Title (Feather Theme) • My Heart Will Go On (Love Theme from 'Titanic') • The Rainbow Connection • Tears in Heaven • A Time for Us • Up Where We Belong • Where Do I Begin (Love Theme).
00311072 P/V/G $12.95

VOLUME 2. JAZZ BALLADS

Autumn in New York • Do You Know What It Means to Miss New Orleans • Georgia on My Mind • In a Sentimental Mood • More Than You Know • The Nearness of You • The Very Thought of You • When Sunny Gets Blue.
00311073 P/V/G $12.95

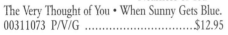

VOLUME 3. TIMELESS POP

Ebony and Ivory • Every Breath You Take • From a Distance • I Write the Songs • In My Room • Let It Be • Oh, Pretty Woman • We've Only Just Begun.

00311074 P/V/G.................................$12.95

VOLUME 4. BROADWAY CLASSICS

Ain't Misbehavin' • Cabaret • If I Were a Bell • Memory • Oklahoma • Some Enchanted Evening • The Sound of Music • You'll Never Walk Alone.
00311075 P/V/G.................................$12.95

VOLUME 5. DISNEY

Beauty and the Beast • Can You Feel the Love Tonight • Colors of the Wind • Go the Distance • Look Through My Eyes • A Whole New World • You'll Be in My Heart • You've Got a Friend in Me.
00311076 P/V/G.................................$12.95

VOLUME 6. COUNTRY STANDARDS

Blue Eyes Crying in the Rain • Crazy • King of the Road • Oh, Lonesome Me • Ring of Fire • Tennessee Waltz • You Are My Sunshine • Your Cheatin' Heart.
00311077 P/V/G.................................$12.95

VOLUME 7. LOVE SONGS

Can't Help Falling in Love • (They Long to Be) Close to You • Here, There and Everywhere • How Deep Is Your Love • I Honestly Love You • Maybe I'm Amazed • Wonderful Tonight • You Are So Beautiful.
00311078 P/V/G.................................$12.95

VOLUME 8. CLASSICAL THEMES

Can Can • Habanera • Humoresque • In the Hall of the Mountain King • Minuet in G Major • Piano Concerto No. 21 in C Major ("Elvira Madigan"), Second Movement Excerpt • Prelude in E Minor, Op. 28, No. 4 • Symphony No. 5 in C Minor, First Movement Excerpt.
00311079 P/V/G.................................$12.95

VOLUME 9. CHILDREN'S SONGS

Do-Re-Mi • The Hokey Pokey • It's a Small World • Linus and Lucy • Sesame Street Theme • Sing • Winnie the Pooh • Won't You Be My Neighbor? (It's a Beautiful Day in This Neighborhood) • Yellow Submarine.
00311080 P/V/G.................................$12.95

VOLUME 10. WEDDING CLASSICS

Air on the G String • Ave Maria • Bridal Chorus • Canon in D • Jesu, Joy of Man's Desiring • Ode to Joy • Trumpet Voluntary • Wedding March.

00311081 P/V/G.................................$12.95

VOLUME 11. WEDDING FAVORITES

All I Ask of You • Don't Know Much • Endless Love • Grow Old with Me • In My Life • Longer • Wedding Processional • You and I.
00311097 P/V/G...................$12.95

FOR MORE INFORMATION, SEE YOUR LOCAL MUSIC DEALER, OR WRITE TO:

HAL•LEONARD® CORPORATION
7777 W. BLUEMOUND RD. P.O. BOX 13819 MILWAUKEE, WI 53213

Visit Hal Leonard online at **www.halleonard.com**
Prices, contents and availability subject to change without notice.